DO THE DEAL

A SIMPLE STEP-BY-STEP METHOD TO BUILD YOUR REAL ESTATE CAREER

RUSTY HAMRICK

Do the Deal: A Simple Step-by-Step Method to Build Your Real Estate Career / Rusty Hamrick —1st ed.

ISBN: 978-0-578-31356-6

CONTENTS

INTRODUCTION

The purpose of this book is to teach you how to attract more clients. I have been a licensed Realtor® since 1999 and what no one told ME in the beginning of my career was my ONLY job is, was, and forever will be, to attract clients. That is it. So here's me, telling you:

Your only job is to attract clients.

- If you have been in the business for 30-plus years, **your only job is to attract clients**.
- Just entering your sophomore season? **Your only job is to attract clients.**
- Brand spanking new, freshly minted license in hand? Especially you, **your only job is to attract clients.**

It's not about "branding" or "websites" or "mindset" or any other buzz words many real estate "gurus" use.

Your **single-minded focus** should be—now and forever" **"What am I doing to attract my next client?"**

Okay, okay. I am being a *little* facetious here. Obviously, there are other skills you will need to develop.

- What do you do during showings?
- How do you complete contracts?
- What is the best way to negotiate each offer?
- How do you present your offer during a multiple offer situation?
- How do you handle yourself during inspections?
- How do you keep the appraiser and the lender in the loop?
- What happens during the escrow/closing process?

We could make a very long list of all the skills required to become a successful real estate agent. But none of those skills matter without clients.

- You can be the best person in the world at marketing houses, but with no willing sellers that won't matter.

- You can run rings around everyone in your office with your descriptions of new listings, but with no buyers to sell them to, who cares?
- Your negotiation skills can rival those of a CIA negotiations expert, but with no deals to negotiate that won't make a big impact on your bottom line.

You are the captain of your real estate ship. Whether you are brand new or a battle-tested veteran, your business drive, vision, and goals must come from you.

If you're new you will soon discover that, as a Realtor®, you occupy all positions in your company—CEO, COO, CFO, administrative assistant, bookkeeper, custodian—and often, babysitter and psychologist too! And as your business grows and you apply time leverage by hiring administrative help and then buyer and seller agents, the workload shifts and evolves from handling clients directly to managing staff. The workload is tremendous and at the end of the day the drive, vision, and goals must STILL always come from you. A tall order, no doubt.

The more you systematize and automate your client interactions and follow-ups, the faster and bigger your business can and will grow.

So, the purpose of this book is to show you how to put into place those systems and habits that will save you time and make you more money. And let's be clear. This is the purpose of our business. I love to help people and find fulfillment in my career through that. But I am also in this business for the paycheck. And it is good and motivating if you are too. So let's do what we can to make that check as big as possible to create as much freedom as we can.

If that sounds good, then read on.

BACKGROUND

In 1999 I was a fresh-faced eager young lad of 23, newly minted license in hand, ready to set all kinds of sales records and make my millions. To set the stage, there were no reality TV shows in 1999 and a significantly smaller number of people had their real estate license. I looked around the business and thought, "Well, I can probably do this! And, you know, THE MONEY!"

I found my way to my first office where I met "Linda," my first manager. She was the best. You could tell there was nothing that was going to ruffle her feathers and there probably wasn't a situation she hadn't dealt with in her career. The perfect balance between drill sergeant and doting mother. She has a response for every situation:

Showing a house with some extreme design choices?

"You just tell them that's why they make 31 flavors!"

Taking clients to a new area that's more in line with their budget?

"Just tell them they'll get more cluck for their buck!"

Clients nervous about putting their home on the market before they've found the next one to purchase?

"You just remind them if you drive past any real estate office in the country you'll never see people and their belongings on the sidewalk out front. You will ALWAYS find people a place to call home, even if it's temporary."

I would hear her say these things, roll my eyes, and think "I'm NEVER going to say that!" Of course, now I say every one of them! I knew I had an amazing person in my corner once I had the clients and was doing the deals. But getting to that point was up to me!

On that first day in my new office, "Linda" handed me the *Caravan Express* (the local magazine where all the new listings were published for our Tuesday Broker's Caravan Open Houses) and said, "Our office is in Area 3 (the Sunset Strip/ Hollywood Hills). You should focus on learning those houses. Good luck!"

That was it—the extent of my training.

It truly was sink or swim time for me. (I sometimes wonder how differently my career would have gone had someone given me the information I'm about to give you!)

It was a super exciting time. The MLS was **just** moving online (we still had listing books!), I was thrilled to be learning a new profession, and I recognized that this was the beginning of a new chapter in my life. I got busy learning my contracts, learning the inventory, learning how to hold open houses, and basically telling anyone and everyone I had ever MET that I was now in REAL ESTATE! I got my first client three weeks after joining my first office, put him in escrow two weeks after that and 60 days later got the biggest paycheck I had ever seen. My career was off to a booming start!

There were two key things I failed to do that would have saved me countless headaches and made me MUCH more money.

1. Keep track of who I was talking to about buying or selling real estate, and
2. Systematically follow up with and refine this group of people.

This is the "secret" to building a successful real estate career. This is what I had been missing and why I am so passionate about this topic now. If you are new in the business or if you are tired of riding the real estate roller coaster—easy street one month, skid row the next—my guess is one of these three steps is lacking:

Step 1: Make a list of every person you've ever met.

Step 2: Communicate with this group consistently over time.

Step 3: Demonstrate value and ask for their business.

Voila! You'll be a millionaire from real estate sales in no time! Sounds easy, doesn't it?

Well, simple at least? Yes.

Easy? No. In practice it can be overwhelming. This is why:

- So many people get their license and never do anything
- So many agents have inconsistent income
- It's easy to tell a professional from a hobbyist

This is also why I decided to write this book. To save you the time and heartache I went through in the early years by showing you how to automate, customize, and systematize as much of your client interactions as possible so you never again drop the ball and miss a new client opportunity. This book is intended as a step-by-step instruction manual to get you started right (or back on track if you've lost focus). I'll share the organizational structure and tools that will help make you a successful Realtor as quickly as possible.

> If you have all the business you want and your client follow-up is buttoned up tight and operating flawlessly, then congratulations! You are clearly an expert in the field! You can close this book and enjoy your hard-won success. If, however, both statements are not true, then keep going.

APPRECIATION MARKETING

This book is focused on appreciation marketing. Building your audience and increasing customer loyalty through strengthening relationships by demonstrating how grateful you are for your customers and their business and referrals is what appreciation marketing is all about. That's quite the mouthful!

The short version? **Give to get.**

Many people have had the experience of Realtors as being shameless self-promotors, slapping our name and logo on every single thing we do. While there is a place for this, there is also a massive opportunity to tone this part down and turn up the gratitude and Thank You Power toward your clients—past, present, and future.

The truth of the matter is today's savvy consumers have so many options to choose from that they are going to work with people who the know, like, trust, AND **remember.** The most effective way to build that trust is to demonstrate your integrity, loyalty, knowledge, and gratitude before they have the opportunity to question it. As an industry we can be known to disappear as soon as the deal is done and the check has cleared. I am embarrassed to admit I have been that agent at times. It's not intentional! It's just the facts and details of the forward moving business can draw our focus away from expressing gratitude consistently over time for past business. The missed opportunity here is that those past clients are our BIGGEST ALLIES when looking for future business! And yet, many of us do next to nothing to care for and nurture those relationships.

In this book I will identify four areas of evergreen business opportunities, starting with the people closest to you and working outward. I will then lay out a step-by-step program for each and offer tools that are incredibly effective to set these programs on autopilot so you don't need to reinvent the wheel every time you need to boost your business. The ultimate goal of these strategies is to level out the ups and downs of the real estate seesaw, the common feast-or- famine experience, so your business runs on continual boost and you determine how far and how big you want to grow!

GETTING IN THE DOOR

There are many great books about marketing (*No BS Marketing to the Affluent* by Dan Kennedy is a personal favorite), negotiating (*Never Split the Difference* by Chris Voss is a hot one right now), and your broker can provide training on local contracts, customs, etc. If they can't, or you're not feeling supported in the way you need, stop reading and call me now. We will get you situated someplace where you CAN be supported and trained properly. This is essential! How can you position yourself as an expert if you don't have the backing, encouragement, and support of your broker?! See the reference guide at the back of this book for my contact info.

This book is not about those things. It is about:

- How to attract clients quickly, easily, and with no drama or hard sell.
- How to fill your pipeline (your upcoming list of clients) with warm leads and contacts so that you are in control of who you work with.
- How to turn on the faucet of business so you can avoid the rollercoaster ups and downs MOST agents deal with in their careers.

If this sounds like a career you would love, one where you get to help who you want and have your referrals arriving on autopilot, then read on.

PRODUCTION SOLVES ALL PROBLEMS

This is a book about how to ATTRACT CLIENTS. Are there other parts to this business? Yes, of course. But without this first crucial step, none of those parts matter.

What does it matter if you've honed your design and staging skills through hours of schooling (and HGTV!) if you don't have a listing to stage?

Who cares if you know the contract inside and out if you don't have anyone to write one for?

Who cares if you're the best negotiator on the planet if you don't have a seller to negotiate for?

Finding sellers and buyers is, was, and should always be your TOP priority. Having more clients will solve most problems.

- If you have a client who isn't performing, driving you up a wall, sucking the life and enthusiasm out of you—but they are your only client—it's tough to let them go.
- If they're one of three it's a little easier to not let them get you down.
- One of 10? Easier still.
- One of an unlimited pipeline? Refer them and refocus on your best, A+, highest dollar clients.

- Those mounting bills with no income coming in? More production would for **sure** help that problem.
- Stuck in your head, afraid to pick up the 10,000-pound phone? Keep a full list of qualified and active sellers and you simply won't have TIME to get stuck in your head.

But none of this is possible without that full pipeline. Filling that pipeline is the aim of this book. Production over perfection, being in action is where you will start to fix these situations.

Gary Keller, in his incredible book *The Millionaire Real Estate Agent*, relays the story of the ceramics teacher. Here is the relevant passage:

> *"David Bayles and Ted Orland in their enlightening book Art & Fear tell the story of the ceramics teacher who divided his class into two groups: One would be graded solely on the quality of their work and the other would be graded solely on the quantity of their work. He was very straightforward about his grading criteria. The group graded on quality would produce one pot, which needed to be perfect to get an A. The quantity group would have all their pots weighed. If they had produced fifty pounds of pots, they got an A. If they produced less, their grade would suffer. The results where [sic] quite revealing. The quality group spent much of*

> *their time planning the perfect pot, but when it came time to create it, they either made mistakes or their skills were too underdeveloped to fulfill their visions. On the other hand, the quantity group churned out pot after pot and, in the process, learned from their mistakes and perfected more advanced techniques. If you haven't guessed, the group that focused on quantity of work not only generated a greater quantity of work but also work of a superior quality."*

Why do I bring this story up? Because real estate is an industry of ACTION—specific and directed action for sure, but action nonetheless. In the words of my coaches Tim and Julie Harris:

"You have to learn to do what you don't want to do when you don't want to do it AT THE HIGHEST LEVEL."

What actions you ask? This book focuses on four specific areas of lead generation.

1. Friends, family, past clients (sphere/circle/tribe marketing)
2. Open houses
3. Expired listings
4. For sale by owners (FSBOs)

These four areas are tried and true evergreen sources of business. They are also the most effective sources and give you the opportunity to build the strongest ties as quickly as possible. I will lay out specific plans and techniques for each category to set you apart from every broker in your area and cement you in people's minds as their go-to real estate pro!

Reach out to me directly for some of the best real estate coaching available. I will put you in touch with my coaches, who are THE BEST!

SPHERE/CIRCLE/ TRIBE MARKETING

According to Google a sphere of influence (SOI) is "a field or area in which an individual or organization has power to affect events and developments." Think of this as everyone you know now, or anyone you have ever met. It can be a bit overwhelming to think of it in these terms and we will go through a process shortly to help you organize them into categories.

This is the process:

1. Define your sphere of influence (SOI)
2. Communicate with your SOI
3. Ask your SOI for their business

The higher the quality of each of these steps, the more money you will make.

It's that simple.

Let's talk about defining your sphere of influence (SOI). From the broadest perspective, think of this as everyone you've ever met. You're probably going to have more influence over the people you have had more consistent and regular contact with (your family or best friend as an example) than you will with your eighth grade math teacher with whom you've haven't spoken in many years! So let's dig a little deeper and define this group a little better. A simple system that is very effective is if you think of people belonging to your A Team, your B Team, and your C Team.

A TEAM

These are your closest associates, friends, family, colleagues, current and past clients.

- Something good happens and you want to tell someone? Add them to your A Team.
- Something tough and you need help? Your A Team.
- Need to take a break and looking for someone to just relax with? Your A Team.

This may not be a big list to start, and that's OK. These are the people you KNOW will call you first, particularly when it comes to real estate needs.

As an example, I have a client who has become a friend. The only thing we ever discuss is real estate. We speak regularly (about once a month) about the goings on in his neighborhood. I know he is married, and I have met his wife once. We have been friends for eight years now. He has referred me nearly $10,000,000 in business over those eight years. He is absolutely on my A Team. Although we don't have a close personal friendship, he knows I am always going to pick up the phone for him and I am his real estate resource. I know when he has a friend who needs help in the real estate arena, I am who he will call. This is an A Team member for sure! Although our friendship is strictly about real estate, he is still a member of my A Team.

B TEAM

The B Team is the next step outside the circle. These are people who you have semi-regular contact with. Truth be told, you will most likely generate the bulk of your business from this group. Unless you are in some specialized situation (your father is THE real estate attorney in town for example, or you husband is the biggest developer in your area), this part of your SOI will strike the perfect balance between frequency of engagement and size of the tribe.

There are only 24 hours in a day. So you need to be strategic about who and how you are engaging with the different members of your SOI. If you have 10 people on your A Team and you spend 30 minutes on the phone with each of them, that is a HUGE chunk of time out of your week. While it may be necessary at times, it isn't generally the best leverage of your time and effort. However, if you can reach 100 members of your B Team in a consistent and systematic way that takes

50% of that time, then you've strategically applied leverage to reach more people in a "nearly as effective" way. One hundred people who think of you as their go-to resource for real estate will have a higher likelihood of interacting with people looking to buy or sell real estate than 10! So the trick is to get yourself known to those 100 (or 20 or 40 or 75) people as quickly and impactfully as possible.

C TEAM

The C Team is the group over whom you will most likely have the least direct influence. These are the people you may be friends with on social media, but you've never had an in-person conversation with. Perhaps it's the cashier at the grocery store who you are friendly with but can't quite remember their name. The person at the gym you've spoken to over the years but have never engaged them in a real estate conversation. These will be your "smile and nod" group so to speak. This can still be a healthy source of referrals IF you know how to engage with them properly. We will discuss that shortly.

Now that you have a little bit of an idea how your SOI is defined, what are you supposed to do with this list? There are two things you need to focus on with this list.

1. Build and refine it

2. Engage and prospect it

That's it. If you were a farmer your sphere of influence would be your field. You need to till the soil, keep the fences in good working order, keep the fertilizer fresh (building and refining the list), plant the seeds, and harvest the crops (engage and prospect the list).

"But how do I do that? It seems like it's so much!"

Not to worry. This is where systems really shine!

EMERGENCY TRIAGE!

Speaking of systems, are you a Realtor who has been in production for a bit and has past clients? Have you ever driven through a neighborhood and seen a For Sale sign in front of YOUR client's house—and it wasn't yours? What systems do you have in place to automate this type of follow-up? Do you have a system in place for consistent follow-up?

In over 20 years of selling real estate, I have never found a system that is easier, more affordable, or more impactful than The Ultimate Closing Gift Real Estate Automation included with the Mailbox Power Executive Membership. This is a 10-touch system that automatically sends a customized gift to your past clients once every 90 days for two-and-a-half years.

You simply add their name to the group. And you're done. For two-and-a-half years!

What type of system do you have in place now? Is it a random collection of phone numbers and emails stored between last year's date book, your memory, and a few Post-it notes? This "system" is costing you money in lost deals!

THIS IS YOUR WAKE-UP CALL! You can have this system up and running within one hour of reading this sentence. That's right—one hour. All of your follow-up concerns can be handled for the next two-and-a-half years within one hour. Simply call the person who sent you this book (or you're welcome to call me—you'll find my contact information at the end of this book) and tell them you want to get set up with The Ultimate Closing Gift Real Estate Automation. Your follow-up will be taken care of so you can get on to the business of growing your database now that your past clients are being nurtured automatically and personally by Mailbox Power.

BUILDING AND REFINING YOUR LIST

Take a piece of paper and write at the top:

MY A TEAM

Who are the 10 people closest to you who are going to help you get your real estate business off the ground? This list may be people who are currently in your life, but it can also be (especially if you're new to the business) your "DREAM TEAM" so to speak.

In a perfect world, who would you want on this list?

This is a subtle but important distinction. It isn't necessarily your 10 best friends (although a close friend or two may be on this list).

- Who in your life are you close with who knows everybody?
- Who in your life are you close with who is already in real estate?
- Who in your life are you close with who interacts with people regularly who are purchasing and selling real estate?
- Who in your life do you have a strong working relationship with who has an extensive network of professional contacts?
- Who in your life belongs to a country club or other social groups and always seems to have the pulse of what is going on?

These are the people you want on your A Team. They have a large list of people they know and are most likely to hear about people with real estate needs first. THIS is your A Team—the people you want to keep in close contact with and nurture those relationships so you stay top of mind.

On a fresh sheet of paper write:

MY B TEAM

Your accountant, your attorney, your friend who is always invited to all the right parties, your dog walker, your dentist, your trainer, your letter carrier, your dry cleaner, your barber or hair stylist, the receptionist at your doctor's office, your children's teachers or principal, the other parents at your children's school, your favorite (or most popular) vendor at the local farmers market, other agents in your office, other agents in your area, your inspectors, appraisers, stagers, photographers—the list could be added to ad infinitum! This is the part that can sometimes seem a little overwhelming, especially in the beginning. But remember, this is just to get you started. You will be continually adding to and refining your lists. Action, action, action! Just start putting people on each list. Your "B Team" will be made up of your Top 100. These are people who you see semi-regularly and make up your network (to use an old-school term).

One way to think of your B Team is, "If I was on an elevator who would I be happy to see walk through the doors?" This is a great place to start. Who are the 100 best people you would want to be in relationship with to help you build the perfect real estate career?

As with your A Team list, these can be people you know or people you would like to know. A portion of your list SHOULD be aspirational because part of this process is about GROWING your lists. There is no hard and fast rule, but most people find it easier to engage with people they already have a relationship with.

So as a guideline, maybe consider the 80/20 rule. This is a phenomenon in all areas of life that says 20% of your effort will generate 80% of your results.

- 20% of the field will generate 80% of the crops.
- 20% of the workforce will generate 80% of the productivity.
- 20% of your sales force will generate 80% of your sales.

This is a universal law, so why not use it here? As a guide, consider putting 80 people you know on your Top 100 and 20 people you would like to know. Don't worry, I'll show you the best ways to engage with these 20 people so they will be not only on your B Team, but many of them will want to be on your A Team as well!

On a fresh piece of paper write:

MY C TEAM

This will be your largest list but the people with whom you have the least influence. They are still an essential part of your list building. These are people who will be moved one day from your C Team to your B Team and a few even to your A Team. These are all the people you come in contact with as you go through the day, both in real life (IRL) and virtually (social media especially).

Part of this exercise is about retraining your world view. You want to start to train your brain to ask the questions:

- Would I want to be in relationship with this person?
- In what way could I contribute to THEIR network?
- What problem do they have that I might be able to solve?
- How can I be of service to this person or group?

This isn't some cold-hearted sorting process. It is just a way to start opening your eyes to the opportunity that is all around us. Group C is about shifting your perspective and realizing just how many people you encounter every single day. There are potential clients everywhere if you know how to look and how to help them get what they need.

"

You can have everything in life you want if you will just help enough other people get what they want.

- Zig Ziglar

So this is a great place to begin to think of how you can contribute to all three of your groups.

Don't spend too much time agonizing over who goes where. The point here is to get into action. You will be living in this (your database) so you can—and will—adjust and refine as you go.

Now that we have a start on our three lists and have begun to define our SOI, the next step is to constantly be adding to and refining this list—tending to your garden so to speak.

- As someone moves out of town (and you sold their house and got a referral fee from the broker who sold them their new house of course!) maybe that person goes from your B Team to your C Team. A resource has moved away BUT you now have a relationship with the agent who helped them buy their new home, so you have a new member of the tribe!
- Your real estate attorney friend has decided it's time to hang up his law license and finally write that novel she's always dreamed of. Still a valuable relationship for sure (long-term and dear friends ALWAYS are) but perhaps this opens more room on your A Team for someone more active in the real estate space.

- You start working on a committee for a fundraiser at your children's school and get to be friends with the Queen Bee of the social world. This super connector (to quote Malcolm Gladwell and his amazing book *The Tipping Point*) can certainly spread the good word at the school about a new and ambitious Realtor.

These relationships are personal because all relationships on some level are personal. I'm not saying you need to become a heartless real estate machine, kicking friends and acquaintances to the curb because they can't contribute to your bottom line! The other side is true too. No one likes to feel pursued or used simply for their social or business connections. But if you can bring a true spirit of service to your friends, colleagues, and your career, then you will have much more success—not to mention fulfillment and happiness—along the way. This is simply a process and a filter to use when you are seeking people who you may help with your service and expertise. Always be asking, "Who can I add to my list that I could contribute to the most and who has the greatest need for my expertise?"

It is a good idea to sit down with your three groups at least once a quarter and decide how they have evolved and what you're going to do to grow and refine them (and thus your real estate career!) in the direction you want.

Now that we have a start on defining our SOI it's time to discuss how we grow. There are several avenues available to us.

The goal is to be constantly improving the quality of the tribe and its membership. By "quality" I am not talking about anyone's inherent worth as a human being!

I mean:

- How likely is this person to want or need to sell or buy a piece of property within the next 90 days?

or

- How likely is this person to KNOW someone who needs or wants to sell or buy a piece of property within the next 90 days?

Think about this: If you had 110 people (every single person on your A Team and every single person on your B Team) who considered you their go-to person for all things real estate you would have more business than you know what to do with.

This should be your first goal when you're evaluating who to add to your SOI.

Here is a list of potential ways to grow your tribe:

1. Phone Calls: Picking up the phone and "dialing for dollars" is one of the most impactful ways you can approach engaging with your tribe. A quick 10-minute call to your top tribe members (your "A Team) four times a year will reinforce to them that you are their go to person for real estate. It is also a great way to add new members to the SOI after you warm them up in person, or with a card and gift.

2. Open Houses. Holding both public and private open houses are a great way to engage with potential buyers and sellers. You can meet people in the neighborhood and include them in your SOI. You can meet other brokers who may have clients for your listings or need help working with buyers in their pipeline. You can meet buyers who are in the market, actively looking at property. We will discuss perfect preparedness for an open house in a later chapter.

Facebook, Instagram, and LinkedIn are fantastic ways to add to your tribe in both an active and a passive way. While books could and have been written about each of these as sales tools, we will look at some techniques later in this book. For now, just know social media can be a great way to brand yourself and your image.

3. Facebook. Think this is just about connecting with friends from high school? Think again. With their highly targeted advertising options, you can select very specific areas and people to add to your tribe. You can then begin to market to them with Facebook Advertising. This is a dramatic oversimplification of course. However, consider your friends list and ask yourself,

"Who on my list do I want on my dream team?"

Create an individualized list of your Top 100 people. You can filter this list so when it's time for Facebook Duty, you look at only those 100 people. Like their photos. Comment on their posts. Engage with them in conversation (proper etiquette says to take a conversation to messenger—do NOT have it back and forth in the comments section for everyone else to read!). This is a great tool for initiating and building relationships.

4. LinkedIn. Think of this as Facebook for professionals. Again, who is your dream team professional referral network? Are they on LinkedIn? LinkedIn provides a place where you can engage with potential SOI members (referral sources) without the confusion of social/professional interactions. LinkedIn is about professionals networking with professionals to create, deepen, and strengthen professional relationships.

5. Instagram. This is an incredible tool for building your brand as a Realtor. Their "photo only" sharing platform allows you to present new listing photos, favorite home collections, brand aesthetics, all with the ability to curate the look and feel of who you are as a person and as a Realtor. There is limited text capability on IG and most conversations are transferred either to DMs (direct messages) or offline for an in-person connection.

These three are the best options for beginning to build a SOI or nurturing an existing SOI with social media. My suggestion would be to pick one and master that, as each has their own flavor and customs for how to engage and what is appropriate behavior. But each has a large enough reach that mastering one could very likely be sufficient (along with other tools we will discuss) to fill your social media business needs.

6. Door knocking. This is one of the most intimidating forms of prospecting out there. For YEARS I was terrified of it. "You want me to knock on a complete stranger's door? **Are you insane?!**" Suddenly visions of snarling attack dogs, giant gates complete with armed guards (I started selling real estate in Beverly Hills don't forget!) and screaming homeowners throwing things at me leapt to mind.

THIS. IS. TERRIFYING. However, statistics tell us this is one of the most effective and fastest ways to generate new business. And if you do it by targeting for sale by owner (FSBO) and expired listings, this will supercharge your prospecting! And, in all the times I have gone door knocking none of the things I was afraid of happening ever did.

There are two main approaches to door knocking:

A. Pick a specific neighborhood you want to dominate and then go door to door, introducing yourself and providing something of value—market reports, flyers for discounts at local businesses, or invitations to a real estate seminar you know of or are hosting are three very common examples. You can really set yourself apart using custom gifts and cards, but more on that later. A neighborhood of about 500 homes will allow you to door knock them four times a year and seems to be the ideally managed amount of properties.

Fears are paper tigers.

—Amelia Earhart

B. Focus on expired listings and FSBOs (more on these later). The difference here is rather than spending time covering a general area repeatedly, you will be identifying those people who have already raised their hands and said they are interested in selling their home.

7. Custom Gifts and Cards. This is the most effective way to establish new relationships and strengthen existing ones. There are many reasons for this.

- The Law of Reciprocity. This basic law of social psychology says that we pay back what we received from others. In other words, give to get.
- It is unique, which sets you apart from the competition.
- It is an upgrade from the tried and true handwritten thank you note.
- It demonstrates a commitment to developing the relationship beyond a generic postcard.

Here are a few ideas:

- How about a "nice to meet you" note with a box of brownies custom baked for your new bestie at your open house?
- Or a water bottle with a picture of your client's house on it, reminding them you are "thirsty for

their referrals"? (Mailbox Power's Executive Membership includes a tool that makes this super easy!)

- Is there someone you'd like to be in conversation with but perhaps they're a little intimidating? Send them a "Chicken List" card and gift as a way to break the ice and warm them as a contact prior to picking up the phone and calling.

The opportunities here are limitless AND unlike anything most people are doing, which is always a way to guarantee you'll stand out. Remember, this is the goal of all the prospecting and marketing we do as agents. People need to know, like, trust, and remember you when it comes time to sell or buy real estate. Nothing ensures this so much as a custom package arriving at your SOI's door.

8. Birthday Automation. Another great way to be in touch with your clients is by enrolling them in a birthday/half-birthday automation. Send them a birthday card AND send them a half birthday card and custom baked mini cake six months before or after their birthday!

Very few people send physical birthday cards anymore. And do you know anyone who sends HALF birthday cards? I use Mailbox Power to manage these automations. It is a simple, powerful, and effective way to show appreciation for your SOI. It is one more way you are showing your appreciation while setting yourself apart from the competition.

OPEN HOUSES

When I was a brand-new Realtor, 50% of my business came from working with people I met at open houses. Open houses can be a fantastic way to meet buyers and sellers, to learn neighborhoods, hear about upcoming listings, and to keep your finger on the pulse of a particular area or neighborhood.

When I say "open house" I'm not talking about showing up to a property you've never been to, dropping an open house sign on the sidewalk and waiting inside for a couple of hours until the time is up. For your open house to be as effective as possible, this is a project that should start the Monday before (if not earlier). There are several steps you should take to super-charge your open house and make your Sunday working hours as productive as possible. Following is the schedule I refined and then used for years for holding Sunday afternoon public open houses.

MONDAY

Choose your open house. It is important you have enough lead time to properly prepare for your open house so the sooner you decide on the property, the better. If you have your own listing(s) and you and your seller have agreed that public open houses are part of the marketing strategy, then your decision is an easy one! If you don't have any listings of your own not to worry. Many agents carry multiple listings and are looking for trustworthy agents in their office or community to host open houses at their listings. Start within your office and see who has new listings. When evaluating listings for open houses remember the public will unconsciously associate you with the property. So as a rule of thumb look for properly priced beautiful houses in the best neighborhoods that are newest on the market! If the ideal property isn't available prioritize this way:

1. Properly priced houses first
2. Best neighborhood second
3. Beautiful houses third

In other words, a properly priced house should be your first priority, then a house in the best location possible, and finally a house in the best condition. A properly priced fixer in an A+ location will generate more traffic and potential business for you than an overpriced beauty next to a freeway. You will be associated with the home by your potential new clients when they meet you, so choosing the right home to hold open is a way to demonstrate you are an expert they can trust. My only caveat here would be this: Action beats theory every time (remember the ceramics teacher) so don't get lost in "analysis paralysis." Make your decision quickly. Pick your house and then move on to the next step.

If you are approaching a listing agent about holding one of their homes open it is a good idea to provide that agent with a list of action items you will be performing on their behalf (use the one at the end of this chapter as a template if you would like) as proof that they can trust you with their listing. Remember, you are asking them to trust you not only with unlocking and locking the door, but also with their reputation in the community, as well as their relationship with the seller. Providing this info can let them know that you understand the responsibility and are equally invested in the process of getting their listing sold. Agents who have many listings frequently have others sit their open houses, so this is a common practice. It is a valuable service you are providing the listing agent as well, IF they can trust their business is being expertly handled. Establishing a secure and trustworthy relationship with a successful listing agent early on can often lead to more reciprocal business (sharing buyers, sharing listings, referrals) in the future.

Now that you have chosen your perfectly priced beautiful listing to sit this coming Sunday, you need to make sure it will be well attended. The best way to do that is to send invitations to the neighborhood, your A Group and your B Group. It is important that the neighborhood and your A Group and B Group know about your open house for two reasons.

> Don't overwhelm people with too many photos in your advertising. Show off the exterior and main interior rooms. Present them in a logical fashion, as you would discover the rooms walking through the house for the first time. Provide enough information so potential buyers are enticed to want to see more. And, maybe skip those closeups of the closets and toilets.

1. Someone in the neighborhood OR your SOI may know someone who wants to buy the house and,

2. You want these people to know you are busy and active in your real estate career. It is a way to invite and include these people while subtly reminding them you're busy selling real estate. It is also another way of going above and beyond that sets you apart from what other agents are doing.

I'll let you in on a little secret as well. MOST listings do not sell because of open houses. That's right. It is a rare occurrence for a buyer to walk in cold with no information about a house, fall in love with it, and buy it. The REAL purpose of public open houses is to allow the agent sitting the house to get to meet people in the area, as well as potential buyers!

So, you want to make sure people in the area are personally invited. Pick the houses closest to your open house (perhaps 10 on either side and 20 across the street) for personal invitations. You can hand-write invitations or use Mailbox Power to send custom designed invitations.

Put a picture of the house you're holding open on the envelope and the front of the card. Put two to three interior "teaser" photos on the inside top, add a short description of the property, and the details of the open house in your message. Using the automation feature and custom merge fields the invitations are addressed individually to the neighbors. Send them on Monday (or the preceding Friday if you are really on top of things!) so they arrive by the end of the week and give people time to plan.

TUESDAY

Time to learn the comps for the house! Start with the MLS and your local title company. There are three areas to focus on:

- All neighborhood comps within the past six to 12 months, regardless of how they compare to the listing you are sitting.
- Comps for the listing you are sitting.
- Alternatives to the listing you are sitting but one price point on either side of the house you are holding open (both more and less expensive).

First, pull all recent sales in the neighborhood. Pull everything that has sold in the past year regardless of whether it is a comparable to your open house. Mr. & Mrs. New Homeowner will be impressed when you can speak knowledgeably about their new property even though it is twice as big and twice as expensive as the one you're holding open. Learn about which properties may have sold outside the MLS via your title company. Another way to cement yourself in the area as the local expert. "Oh yes, 1234 Main Street was a quiet sale so it never came to market. But it's an excellent comp for this house because...."

Second, pull the specific comps for the property you are holding open. Mr. Nosy Neighbor may show up with opinions on pricing and you will need to hold your own in that discussion if you claim to be the neighborhood expert!

Third, look for homes that might be good alternatives that are a little bit less and a little bit more expensive than the one you are holding open. You can go to a broader geographic area to find these. Your priority is to sell the house you are sitting but if it becomes **very clear** that this isn't the house for someone (too expensive, not enough bedrooms, etc.) a **fantastic** way to pick up new clients is by rattling off three or four alternatives that you would be **happy** to show to your new prospective clients.

Check out the new listings board if your office has one. And ask the agents who tend to list a lot of homes if they have anything coming up. You'll really shine in a client's mind if you're able to get them into a property before anyone else!

After this research at your desk is complete it's time to get in the car and drive the neighborhood. Drive the comps and look at them from the outside. Notice how close they are to busy streets, or if they have especially good curb appeal. Is there a school nearby, or does the house sit under a flight pattern? This research serves double duty. First, you are preparing yourself for your public open house. And second you are learning the market in general. Nothing is a waste of time here. There have been countless times I've been able to speak intelligently about a particular part of town because of the open house research I had done years earlier. To position yourself as an expert, you must become an expert!

WEDNESDAY

Now that you know the neighborhood comps, Wednesday is the perfect day to learn alternative options to the house you'll be sitting. Many people use Sunday open houses as a sort of "wishful planning" session. They're in the market for a starter two-bedroom but they say, "Oh, let's just see what the big four-bedroom around the corner is like!" Or they know one day they are planning to move to the swankiest part of town so why not go see it now?

My experience has been that on Sundays people often look one price point above where they actually intend to purchase. So, figure out what that price point would be and learn three or four alternatives you can offer as suggestions. Choose one or two currently on the market and ESPECIALLY one or two that may NOT be on the market currently.

These can be listings you know are coming through your office, unrepresented sellers you have come across through your FSBO and expired marketing, or just neighbors you've met in your various open house door knocking sessions. It is irresistible to buyers hearing about something secret or hidden, and that is how off-market listings are perceived.

A couple of words of caution. First, your job as the representative of the seller (whether it's your listing or someone else's) is to sell their house. It can cause many problems if you have not exhausted this possibility before you start pitching other properties to prospective clients, particularly if they happen to know the sellers! However, if for whatever reason it is clear the house you're sitting is not the right fit (too many stairs, not big enough, no yard, etc.), then you want to be prepared with a few alternatives. This will help cement you in their minds as the neighborhood expert.

And second, don't be so eager to show off your knowledge of secret pocket listings that you miss the buying signs toward the house you're sitting! These two go hand in hand, so be attentive to the fact that your first priority is to sell the house you're holding open. If that is a definite impossibility, then go for it and pick up your new buyers!

And Wednesday is the day to learn those properties you can use to entice these prospective new clients with your expertise. Identify them, drive by, see if you can get into the houses. Maybe you can piggy-back on an already scheduled showing? Or perhaps the house is on a lockbox? Come Sunday you want to be as knowledgeable about them as possible!

THURSDAY

Enjoy a little open house downtime before the big weekend push! Perhaps skip ahead to the FSBO or expired marketing sections in the book and implement some of the strategies mentioned there. Then, head back here on Friday.

FRIDAY

Start the day by creating your "Open House Nice to Meet You" open house automation in Mailbox Power. Link the "I Need Your Mailbox" link for this group to a QR code. Put the code on a flyer to place next to the sign-in sheet. Here is the specific way to design the card:

1. Put a picture of the house on the front of the card.
2. Put interior photos of the house on the inside top part of the card.
3. Write the following message on the bottom half of the card:

   Dear [[firstname]],

   It was such a pleasure meeting you at the property at [[merge1]] this past Sunday! YOu may remember this INSERT SHORT PROPERTY DESCRIPTION HERE. If you have any questions about this or any other fine homes in our area, I would enthusiastically assist you with your needs!

4. Include your phone number, email, and logo on the back of the card.
5. BONUS: Include a QR code linking to a property video, or an intro video of what benefits you provide to your clients!

You'll use this automation in two different ways. First, when people arrive and you ask them to sign in let them know they can either fill out the paper form or scan the QR code and input their information on their phone. Create a giveaway (a customized BBQ tool set laser-engraved with the winner's name is a personal favorite) as added incentive to use the QR code.

The second way you'll use this automation is when you are door knocking and REALLY connect with people at the open house. You can use the Mailbox Power App to add them to this specific automation. The system will then send your guests a card and brownies and you will ABSOLUTELY stand out in their mind as the go-to Realtor in the neighborhood.

Once your "Nice To Meet You Automation" is in place it's time to get out and meet the neighbors. Pick the houses closest to your open (perhaps 10 on either side and 20 across the street) and door knock the neighborhood. If you mailed invitations, this should be the same list. Their invitations should have arrived by Friday and this is the perfect conversation starter. "Hi, I'm Mary Jane Doe with eXp Realty. I wanted to make sure you received my invitation to the open house I'll be holding Sunday at 1234 Main Street?" This is a great opportunity to meet the neighbors and demonstrate the level of effort you are willing to put into selling an open house. People will remember you for this.

One of the most lucrative things you can do to plant the seed that you are the neighborhood expert is to follow up with every person you meet while you are door knocking. Mailbox Power makes this possible to take care of "on the fly." After you've connected with a homeowner, simply add their name and address (easy to know since you'll be standing at their front door) to the "Nice to Meet You" automation you just created. Most likely the homeowner will forget about your meeting UNTIL they receive a card and brownies in the mail from you. Nothing else will set you apart from the competition the way this one little tip will.

Try to keep your conversations quick (just popping by to invite you to the open house this Sunday!) and to the point (remember, you are a busy professional with a long list of things to take care of) and then it's on to the next house! You should be able to door knock the neighbors in a couple of hours.

If no one is home when you arrive, you have two options.

1) Bring something to leave behind—a printed flyer for the property, a neighborhood market analysis, or an invitation to the Sunday open house are all good ideas. Pick one.

2) Use the Mailbox Power App to add them to the "Open House Nice to Meet You automation." You can add their info while standing on their front steps and then your follow-up is taken care of. When they receive the package, they will often call to ask about the open house (whether they attended or not!). This is the perfect conversation starter and a great way to meet and engage with more neighbors in the 'hood!

SATURDAY

Today is the day to review your comparable information, print your sign in sheets, prepare your open house signs (make sure they are clean and the property address is easy to read from the street), and make sure you are ready to go for Sunday! Take a drive through the neighborhood one more time to see what is going on. Often it looks the same, but you don't want to be caught off guard if someone asks about a major change you didn't see because you haven't been in the area recently. Make sure the alternative options you have selected are still available and haven't sold. If they are under contract, see what you can find out from the listing agent so you can be informed should someone bring up that particular property during the open house. Make sure you are ready to go for Sunday!

SUNDAY

TODAY IS THE BIG DAY! I know it can seem like a lot of preparation, but it pays off. When you start to be known as the Open House Queen (or King) by making sure you take all these steps, you will have your choice of listings, and clients will be eager to work with someone so detail-oriented, knowledgeable, and thorough. This level of preparation will also bolster your confidence as the area expert. You must be the expert before you can show others you are!

Begin the day with a nutritious breakfast and pack a snack for a little later. There likely won't be much time for food once

When you arrive at the house don't put your last open house sign up yet! Buyers consider this a, *"Yes, come in! We are ready for you!"* sign and you don't want to turn someone away because you're not ready. Leave the sign down and the door closed while you get the house ready. When the scene is set, unlock the front door and place the open house sign, welcoming your many new clients.

things get rolling. Determine when you want to arrive at the property. I recommend a minimum of 30 minutes before the open house is scheduled to begin to properly prepare the home. Here is a useful rundown of items to check:

- Make sure every light in the house is on, regardless of how bright and sunny it may be outside.
- Open windows and doors (or have them closed and AC/heat on).
- Have music playing. Pick something that complements the style of the house or potential buyer.
- Make sure there are no dishes in the sink.
- Clear counters of extraneous debris and items.
- Make sure toilet lids are down.
- Lock away valuables and medications.
- Light candles.

Remember, many buyers show up early so they can be the first person through the door. Arrive early enough to take a few minutes and prepare yourself mentally to "put on a show." Being sweaty, out of breath, and harried from showing up late and having prospective clients watch you frantically try to get everything open and ready is no way to make a professional impression (he writes from experience—ha!).

Once you determine when to arrive at the property, backtrack how long it will take you to place your signs. Add 15 minutes. Trust me, it is better to arrive at a property early and make a few follow-up calls from the car than it is to be the last person to arrive and unlock a cold, dark house in front of a group of irritated strangers.

Again, I'm not just guessing here. Learn from my experience. Take the time you need to position the signs properly. Make sure you follow all area sign requirements and restrictions. I knew a broker here in Los Angeles who used to put out 25 to 30 signs for every open house. They eventually became a nuisance and created more bad will than positive advertising. Be mindful of the fact that you are in someone's neighborhood. It is a business opportunity for you, but it's also where people (often your clients) are living their lives. Don't be the oblivious jerk with no regard for other people!

When you are preparing the house, turn on every light and lamp in the house. Do this even if it is bright and sunny outdoors and the house is already well lit. It helps to bring a sense of life to each room when people enter.

Make sure the kitchen is clean (yes I have washed dirty dishes to clear the sink and so should you—and then ask the owners to make sure the sink is clear for all subsequent showings and open houses), the candles are lit, the blinds are open, the doors are unlocked, the toilet seat lids are down, the music is playing, your heartbeat is calm, your clothes are neat and professional, your sign-in sheet and property brochures are ready, and THEN you can begin to deal with the public.

DURING THE OPEN HOUSE

Now is your time to shine. It is time to put all your preparation to work and show the public you are the trusted expert, and they would be smart to put their trust in you.

One of the best skills you can master is being able to meet people where they are. (Buying Styles by Michael Wilkinson is a great book about identifying the four types of buying styles and how best to engage each type. See the reference page at the end for more information). As a prospective client approaches the property ask yourself, how should I greet them? Are they shy and timid? A gentle, warm, welcoming approach would be best. A boisterous group being led by their brash Realtor? Let's get the party started! And remember, never judge a book by its cover! Too many times I have seen the shy, reserved person who barely says a word end up making an offer while the loud "this is my house!" person walks out the door, never to be heard from again.

Your job is to create the environment so people can explore the house in their own way and begin to picture themselves in the house—to "emotionally move in." That can be a difficult process for people when the listing agent is hovering and following them around the house. You want to be accessible, without being creepy; attentive without smothering them. I have found a hands-off approach can be most effective.

You might say something like "Hi, I'm Rusty. Thanks for coming. We have four bedrooms, three bathrooms, and are asking $475,000. Don't miss the bonus room off the master. We're here until 5 p.m., so check it out, take your time, and if you have any questions, just holler!"

SIGNING IN

There was a time when I forced people to sign in as soon as they walked through the door. This often created more frustration than it was worth and I'm sure I lost potential clients because of this initial friction. If the seller or listing agent is requiring this, there's not much you can do of course. But in that case say something like, "The seller has requested that everyone who comes through the door sign in so they have a record of who was in their home." Going to open houses can be a way for people to shop for their next home, a way to see what their property value might be, or just a way to spend some time on an afternoon. I specifically use the word HOME to emphasize to people that, although the sellers have opened their doors, it is a home first and should be treated as such. Ninety-nine percent of people will understand this and sign in.

If you're just trying to get everyone to sign in because you're hunting for their information, then forcing it out of someone who doesn't want to give it will never generate a

> If you watch people sign in, often their handwriting gets much better. Don't be afraid to ask people if you can't read what they've written. Heaven forbid there is an issue later—you want to make sure you have a useful record of everyone who came through the property.

client you want to work with. I believe in the "more flies with honey" method. Sometimes people prefer to sign in when they're leaving (after they've established a little rapport with you). Don't try to convert every single person who walks through the door.

Keep track of all the visitors of course, but when filtering for new clients look for the people who you have a vibe with; the people who you would enjoy working with, whatever your reason. I know some agents who LOVE working with first time home buyers. I know other agents who only want to list properties in a particular neighborhood. I know agents restarting their career who only want to work with buyers or sellers who need to complete a transaction in the next 30 to 90 days, and still others who are only interested in working a particular price point.

Whatever your criteria (if you are new, don't be too picky here!), keep your eyes peeled for those people. Keep a record of everyone who comes through, but make sure to follow up with "your" people in particular.

After a few open houses it will become pretty clear. Once you've identified these people your job is to cement yourself in their mind as their real estate expert. This is a process, so don't feel pressured to have them buy the house you're holding open. Remember, your primary purpose during the open house is to sell the house you are holding open. If, however, it becomes clear that it is not the right house for your potential clients then it is appropriate and acceptable to begin to talk to them about other houses that might work for them, both on the market and off. If you have done your job in the week prior to the open house and prepared diligently, this is really a time to wow them with your detailed market knowledge.

Interacting face to face is only half of the process though. Chances are your new perspective clients will be seeing multiple houses during the open house window. In addition to wowing them with your product knowledge, you also need to stand out from every other Realtor they are meeting. Don't forget, people work with people they know, like, trust, and remember!

Read that last sentence again. Here it is:

PEOPLE WORK WITH PEOPLE THEY KNOW, LIKE, TRUST, AND REMEMBER!

This last part is perhaps the most essential piece of everything we have been talking about in this book. It doesn't matter if people know like and trust you if, when it comes time to list or buy real estate, they forget to call you! One technique I have found particularly effective here is to be in enthusiastic communication with them the week following the open house. Once again, nothing beats Mailbox Power for accomplishing this.

When you have connected with someone and you want to wow them with your follow-up, either have them scan the QR code flyer you created on Friday, or manually add them to the "Open House Nice to Meet You" automation in the Mailbox Power app.

People are sometimes grateful, sometimes confused, sometimes indifferent *in the moment.* But here is the magic of this technique. They leave the open house and forget about you, the house, the other houses they've seen, etc. Monday, their phone and email is inundated with calls and messages from everyone they met on Sunday. "Ugh!" they say. "I did not sign in just so I could be hounded by these people!" Then Tuesday or Wednesday they go to their mailbox and find a greeting card and brownies. When they open it, BOOM there is a photo of the house where you met as well as your contact info!

I guarantee this will set you apart and make you stand out in their mind. And that is really what all of the lead generation, prospecting, and marketing we all do is all about. **Set yourself apart!** To do this, you have to do what no one else is doing. This is a simple and efficient way to stand out. This also takes care of your post-open house follow-up **during** the open house. Monday is not spent hounding anyone on the phone or having to write cards or emails. The follow-up is created in real time and then the system does the work automatically.

Again, this is not for every single person who comes through the house. But for those people you connect with, who you really want to work with, this is the most powerful way to set yourself apart and establish yourself as the area expert.

AFTER THE OPEN HOUSE

Once the open house is finished, it is vital that all lights are off, doors and windows are closed and locked, candles are out, and the house is in better condition than when you arrived.

Check in with your seller, or the listing agent with a status update. Do not—I repeat, do not—tell them someone is writing an offer or is interested or wants to come back this week. If people have said that AND they follow through, then you can have that conversation. If, however, they were excited in the heat of the moment and ultimately decide to do nothing then you will be left with a disappointed seller and a bit of egg on your face.

"What about those people who said they are writing an offer?" Or, "Did you ever hear from the people who said they wanted to come back?"

It is better to provide facts and figures. "Hi there, we're all closed up here. We had 17 people through. Several people asked about our pricing strategy (indicate if the impression was too high, too low, or about right). Many people really love the backyard. Some people questioned the impact of the proximity to such a busy street/power lines/flight path, etc." It is important the seller receive a no-nonsense realistic picture of what went on at the open house and how the public is responding to their home.

When you leave the property make sure you pick up all your open house signs. Nothing will make a neighborhood sour on your brand faster than excessive open house signs strewn about the area. Placing them a few hours before the open house shows you are proactive and engaged in selling a property. A few hours (or days!) after an open house says you don't care about how your presence affects a neighborhood. Spend the extra time to diligently collect your signs.

Then head home for some relaxation before instituting this system again tomorrow!

OPEN HOUSE CHECKLIST

__ Choose open house.

__ Send invites to 40 of the closest neighbors.

__ Door knock and personally invite 40 of the closest neighbors.

__ Know and speak intelligently about the comparables as it relates to pricing strategy.

__ Customized visitor follow-up cards and brownies.

__ Digital and paper sign-in sheet for a thorough record of attendees.

__ Extensive open house signage throughout the neighborhood, placed and removed the day of the open house.

__ Custom soundtrack to complement the style of the property.

__ Thorough follow-up with you and/or the sellers post-open house.

EXPIRED LISTINGS

One of the richest veins of business that can be mined in the real estate business is unrepresented sellers, aka expired listings. Before we dive into the specific technique I have used to great effect, I want to take a moment to talk about effectiveness in marketing and prospecting. This is hard work. It is physically demanding to show houses all day. It is mentally taxing to remember all the facts and figures of the listings and ongoing deals, not to mention remembering all the people we interact with as well as the pertinent details about them and their lives. It is emotionally demanding as we help other people navigate what is often the biggest financial decision they've ever made.

Add to this the myriad personal situations that could necessitate the need to move (change of job, divorce, marriage, births, deaths) and, as you are no doubt aware dear reader, we often play the role of psychologist, counselor, disciplinarian, and teacher— all in one afternoon! And this is just in handling our ongoing business. It is against this backdrop that we are then expected to generate new business. In fact, let me flip that around. This is the backdrop against which we must generate new business. Generating new business is our first and most important priority always and forever! The reason I am pointing this out now is that expired prospecting can be one of the most lucrative AND most challenging ways to prospect for new business out there. I have taken many courses, read countless books, worked with coaches and managers to attack expireds as a source of business. Here is what I have learned.

The most consistent advice is to door knock unrepresented sellers (expired) the day the listing contract expires, as early in the day as possible. I have seen people recommend going as early as 7 a.m. I have done this. My experience was awful. No one ever threw anything at me, or screamed at me, or chased me off their porch while waving a broom around. But the anxiety I experienced the night before I was going to go door knocking as well as while I was door knocking was overwhelming.

The few times people did come to the door the conversations never lasted more than two to three minutes. Usually no one would answer the door and I would see eight to 10 packets on the doorstep that look remarkably similar to my own. So, I'd leave my packet, get in the car and head to the next one.

I picked a fairly large geographic area so this ended up being a time-consuming and discouraging process that never netted me any business. I know why this is. I found the experience so tortuous that I didn't do it consistently enough over a long enough time for it to bear fruit.

And this is the equation for how to be successful when marketing and prospecting.

Consistency + time = results

A question you must be very honest with yourself about is, "What activities can I be consistent about?" If every time you wake up you DREAD what you are about to go do, one of two things will happen: Either you'll stop doing what you are dreading or you'll create a life you hate. Neither of these outcomes is ideal!

Now, if you are someone who is built to knock on doors at all hours of the day and night, CONGRATULATIONS! You have access to one of the most lucrative ways to generate listings in the real estate industry. I would direct you to TimandJulieHarris.com They are my real estate coaches and have wonderful training and motivation.

I would make the argument that something you will do with 90% consistency that is 50% effective is BETTER than something you will do with 20% consistency that is 90% effective. So, if you are like me and simply not built to knock on doors, then you will find tremendous value in the system I lay out in the following pages.

And yes, Tim Harris, I understand that much of real estate is "learning to do what you don't want to do when you don't want to do it at the highest level." That being said, I have found that for myself, the following system is the highest and best use of my time because it allows me to prospect a large number of unrepresented sellers for a long period of time and has generated results profitable enough to justify saving me the anxiety of door knocking at 7 a.m.!

There are several benefits to using this system.

- I actually use it! The best system in the world doesn't make a difference if you're not putting it into practice.
- It allows me to follow up with a large number of prospects over the course of several weeks, so I am continually planting the seeds for upcoming listings.
- It is a "set it and forget it" system. Once I have begun the drip automation the system follows up on my behalf without me having to do anything.
- It allows me to go back in time and find houses that did not sell in the past and add them to the list. I have made quite a bit of money selling houses that were listed three to seven years prior to today but never sold.

This is a numbers game. Whether you are visiting the houses in person, calling them, or mailing to them, you will need to be in touch with many sellers over many weeks to get the results you are looking for. This is not a get-rich-quick system, nor is it a system that you can turn on and off and expect maximum results. But if you are willing to put in dedicated time every day then you will see results.

The system I have built is a 12-week card and letter automation, and it is run completely with Mailbox Power. I used to do this by hand and, although it was time-consuming, the results made the time invested worth it.

So you do NOT need to have a Mailbox Power account to implement this system (it just makes it easier AND allows for some extra bells and whistles). I'll break the system down for you over the next few pages.

A quick formatting note. The following letters have been adjusted so each letter will fit on a single page of this book. When I send the automation, either by hand or with Mailbox Power, all the letters are printed on standard business-sized stationery and sent in business-size envelopes.

DAY 1

Custom 5X7-inch card with a photo of their house on the envelope and on the cover of the card. The message on the inside is printed on the next page.

I include a QR code that takes the viewer to a YouTube video of me explaining why I am sending them a card rather than knocking on their door.

The back of the card has a list of my top sales along with photos of the houses and my contact information.

I keep a blank version of this card in my "Saved Projects."

TOP OF CARD

Did you know there are only three reasons your home did not sell?

1. The Price. Simply put, this is the most crucial element in selling a property. I will provide a comprehensive market overview so you can fully understand all factors at play when YOU decide what price you want to ask for your property.

2. The Product. This is the location, condition, curb appeal, and desirability of your property. We will work together to highlight its strengths, minimize its weaknesses, and help your property put its best foot forward to prospective buyers.

3. The Promotion. Even homes that are properly priced

and in turn-key condition fail to sell. Why? The home was marketed properly to drive the right traffic swiftly enough to generate interest and then an offer. My "full court press" marketing strategy will ensure maximum exposure for maximum results.

BOTTOM OF CARD

Dear [[firstname]],

What went wrong? Your property should have sold.

I recently saw your home at [[merge1]] is no longer listed for sale within the MLS. If you are still interested in selling, I can help. We are experiencing an incredible shortage of properties to sell. Buyers are clamoring for nearly every new property that comes on the market IF it is positioned properly.

If you are disappointed your property didn't sell, I want you to know I understand. I am excited for the opportunity to help you solve this challenge and help you participate in this, the hottest real estate market we have ever seen in Los Angeles. Call or text me today and let's set up a no-pressure, free, confidential consultation.

Your success is my success.

All the best,

DAY 4

First business sized letter and envelope, introducing what you can offer to the seller. Always remember, people don't care what you can do. People care what you can do FOR THEM. These letters are where you will lay out some of your unique selling propositions.

Dear [[firstname]],

What went wrong?

It is natural to ask this question when your home fails to sell the first time around. Although it may seem as though every house is flying off the shelves in multiple offers right now, rest assured that you are not alone.

So what's next? If you are looking for a fresh approach to getting your home sold why not give me a call today? I specialize in helping sellers position their home to generate showings and, more importantly, **offers**. A few key aspects of my unique marketing approach are to provide my sellers with:

Total Market Overview – An in-depth analysis of your competitive position in the marketplace.

Curb Appeal Review – An honest assessment of your home's curb appeal and how to improve it.

Staging Consultation – A detailed review of how your home can better appeal to a buyer.

Marketing Plan Analysis – A thorough evaluation of your marketing strategy to expose your home to the maximum number of buyers.

More of the same will not work.

You deserve to sell your home. I offer my clients unmatched personal service, attention to detail, and clear communication. To explore a new approach to selling your home call me—or send me a text—for your FREE and CONFIDENTIAL evaluation.

Your success is my success.

All the best,

DAY 7

Time for another card. This one explains the relationship between supply, pricing, product quality, and marketing and how they all affect the time a house will stay on the market.

TOP OF CARD

Why Did Your Home Listing Expire Unsold?

The Market /Property Profile Formula

$$\text{TIME ON MARKET} = \frac{\text{SUPPLY + PRICE}}{\text{PRODUCT QUALITY + MARKETING}}$$

- If the supply of homes increases without a corresponding increase in demand, the time your home stays on market will increase.

- If you increase the price, the time on market will increase. If you decrease it, the time on market will decrease.

- If the quality of your home (appearance, staging, cleanliness, paint, maintenance) increases, the time on market will decrease.

- If the quality of marketing increases, the time on market will decrease.

BOTTOM OF CARD

When you've kept your home show ready, left for showings, and anticipated an offer for months, it can be quite frustrating when your home listing expires without a sale. It's tempting to want to place blame on ineffective marketing, your listing agent, the market, or other factors. It could be an of these, or a combination. This formula keeps things straightforward and analytical.

These statements are generalizations, but the ratios are such that increasing anything on the top will increase Time On Market, while increasing anything on the bottom will DECREASE Time On Market. While you can't control the market, you DO have control over Pricing, Product Quality, and Marketing.

Call me today and let's see how we can put this control to some USE and get your property sold. Your success is my success.

All the best

DAY 10

For the first 10 days we have sent a series of cards and letters to get their attention. The next several touches we will continue to drip on them, providing relevant information and asking pertinent questions designed to get them to pick up the phone and call you.

Dear [[firstname]],

Your home should have sold.

The market is stronger than ever and homes are selling in record time for record prices. So what happened? Why did your home fail to sell when other homeowners like you have been able to move on with their lives? The answer is simply having the right marketing to properly expose your home to every available buyer in the marketplace. More exposure equals a faster sale at a higher price. Take a look at just a few of the ways I position my listings to receive more showings and more offers:

- Custom pricing and marketing evaluation
- Quality photos, video, and virtual tour
- Email to my 20,000-plus person list reaching the most active agents, lenders, and buyers in the market today
- Targeted social media (Facebook, Instagram, Twitter) advertising
- In-person showings handled by me, not an unspecified "team member"

Your home is unique; you deserve a unique marketing plan. Let me put my expertise to work to generate an offer on your home today. To explore a new approach to selling your home call me—or send me a text—for your FREE and CONFIDENTIAL evaluation.

Your success is my success.

All the best,

DAY 17

For the first 10 days we have sent a series of cards and letters to get their attention. The next several touches we will continue to drip on them, providing relevant information and asking pertinent questions designed to get them to pick up the phone and call you.

Dear [[firstname]],

If you had to pick one reason why your home didn't sell the first time what would it be?

Often the reason a home doesn't sell is because it wasn't properly positioned to attract the maximum number of potential buyers. The combination of pricing, marketing, showing, and negotiating strategies was not optimal and the result is your property failed to sell.

So, what is the solution?

I provide my clients with an in-depth analysis of their home's competitive position in the marketplace. This is not simply a list of comparables. This is a total market overview that will provide you with a complete and accurate assessment of how buyers view your property's asking price, its condition and location, and its benefits and challenges relative to the competition.

The report is free and is part of a no-obligation consultation I provide to all of my sellers when they are considering marketing their home. You've heard the phrase, "If it ain't broke don't fix it." The opposite is true, too. Call me to learn how you can sell your property quickly and profitably.

I am here to help you move you on to the next chapter in your life.

Call me—or send me a text—for your FREE and CONFIDENTIAL evaluation.

Your success is my success.

All the best,

DAY 24

For the first 10 days we have sent a series of cards and letters to get their attention. The next several touches we will continue to drip on them, providing relevant information and asking pertinent questions designed to get them to pick up the phone and call you.

Dear [[firstname]],

Are you simply one of many?

I recently reached out because your home was listed in the MLS for sale but never sold. This must be a frustrating experience, especially in light of all the evidence that the market is "hot, hot, HOT!"

The truth is that homes often don't sell because they aren't marketed SPECIFICALLY. Some agents carry many listings, feeling no pressure to sell any specific house. The pressure is relieved because they have many other listings and they know eventually a certain number of them will sell.

But YOU are left to wonder what happened? Where are my multiple offers? Why didn't my house go over asking? What did we do wrong?

I am here to get you back on track and maximize your profit from your property. My 22 years of experience in the Los Angeles real estate market means I will adapt to YOUR specific needs. Each house is unique, and every seller has their own situation that must be handled with care and understanding. I have the market knowledge and the sales experience to back it up.

Isn't it time for you to take advantage of this market, cash out, and move on with your life? Give me a call or shoot me an email for your FREE and CONFIDENTIAL evaluation.

Your success is my success.

All the best,

DAY 31

For the first 10 days we have sent a series of cards and letters to get their attention. The next several touches we will continue to drip on them, providing relevant information and asking pertinent questions designed to get them to pick up the phone and call you.

Dear [[firstname]],

"How can I make selling my house a positive experience?"

Many sellers who have previously had a bad experience with the real estate market (or their agent!) are reluctant to believe they can have a positive experience. They don't want to let themselves believe they could receive market value for their property, let alone a multiple offer situation. They would prefer to not ponder what their lives would be like had they been able to sell their property when it was first listed. Ask yourself these questions:

- What would my life look like if I am able to sell my house in the next 45 days?
- How would my life change if I had the equity OUT of my home and INTO my bank account?
- What dreams am I not fulfilling because I have not been able to sell my house?

Give me a call and we can work together with a great tool—the Seller's Estimated Net Sheet. This will give you an idea of how you'll profit if you sold your house today.

I am here to help you answer these questions and move you on to the next chapter in your life.

Call me—or send me a text—for your FREE and CONFIDENTIAL evaluation.

Your success is my success.

All the best,

DAY 38

For the first 10 days we have sent a series of cards and letters to get their attention. The next several touches we will continue to drip on them, providing relevant information and asking pertinent questions designed to get them to pick up the phone and call you.

Dear [[firstname]],

Would you like to sell your home in the next 30 days? It's Rusty again, reminding you I specialize in helping people who may be frustrated that their property didn't sell the first time around.

Just one example of my marketing plan is the effective use of the internet and digital marketing to maximize exposure for your home. This is absolutely critical, as 86% of buyers today use the internet as their primary information resource. In addition, when working with sellers I offer my clients:

- Complete market overview and pricing analysis
- Online advertising on Facebook, Instagram, Redfin, Zillow, Twitter, Realtor.com
- Extensive and consistent email distribution to my 20,000-plus member email list
- Enhanced MLS listing with a linked virtual tour and property website
- Leveraged personal marketing through long term local broker relationships

If you are considering re-listing your property, I would welcome the opportunity to interview for the job.

Call me now.

Isn't it time for you to take advantage of this market, cash out, and move on with your life? Call me—or send me a text—for your FREE and CONFIDENTIAL evaluation.

Your success is my success.

All the best,

DAY 45

For the first 10 days we have sent a series of cards and letters to get their attention. The next several touches we will continue to drip on them, providing relevant information and asking pertinent questions designed to get them to pick up the phone and call you.

Dear [[firstname]],

What would your life look like today if you had sold your home when you first put it on the market?

If the only thing holding up your dreams is the sale of your home, wouldn't you agree that it may be time for a fresh approach, a new direction, and a new set of eyes? As a real estate professional who specializes in marketing homes that have previously been on the market, I can help you attract more buyers. Did you know:

- Generation X and Y (Millennials) use the internet as their primary information resource. They don't pick up the paper or read real estate guides. Nearly all of their research is done online and via social media.

- According to the National Association of Realtors, Millennials (ages 25 to 40) are the largest group of homebuyers in the marketplace today, comprising 37% of the home buying public

- Facebook and Instagram are, for many, their primary means of discovering new neighborhoods and new listings.

- Sites such as Zillow and Redfin (flawed though their algorithms may be) are also one of the primary locations home buyers research the market before, during, and after their transaction.

Having an agent fluent in these platforms and advertising modes is essential in today's market. I am a different type of real estate professional. We really should talk as soon as possible. Call or text me and we can schedule a quick, free, easy consultation.

Your success is my success.

All the best,

DAY 52

We have now been in touch with our prospective client for nearly two months. This is the last card I send to let them know that I am available, but I also need to stay focused on those people who are ready and willing to sell their real estate now.

Dear [[firstname]]

As a dedicated real estate professional, I have the luxury of living in the real estate market day in and day out, becoming exquisitely aware of market changes on a day-to-day basis. With all the noise coming from national media outlets, social media and the internet, as well as neighbors, family and friends, it can be difficult for you, someone not in the market on a minute-by-minute basis, to get a good handle on what is ACTUALLY happening in the real estate market.

This is the tenth week I've reach out and it will be my last attempt. Should you, or anyone you know, ever have any questions about the real estate market I would ENTHUSIASTICALLY assist you with your needs.

All the best,

HOW TO IMPLEMENT THIS AUTOMATION

Create a blank 5x7 custom card with the messaging you would like to include. My first touch includes a QR code to a video explaining why I'm mailing them and not banging on their door at 8 a.m. Leave the front of the card and the envelope blank. Keep this in your saved projects.

Create a 5x7 greeting card with your logo on the front (or, if you have an Executive Membership with Mailbox Power use the Photo Merge feature to put a photo of their house on the front of the card. Personalization and automation are tremendous influencers!) and the third touch message on the inside. Mine includes a "FORMULA FOR SELLING" chart explaining how pricing and time on market are directly related.

I have seven additional letters and send one per week for the next seven weeks.

My final touch is a greeting card explaining I've now been in touch for eight weeks with no response and, although I am available should they have any questions or real estate needs in the future, I need to keep my focus on those most committed to selling their homes now.

Create an automation entitled "Expired Listing Marketing," which includes all the letters and cards EXCEPT the first card, because the first card needs to have the visuals customized to each individual house.

This is the "sitting at your desk how to" of actually working through adding people to this automation.

1. Determine which homes you will be prospecting.
2. Locate and save a photo of the home (drive by, Google images, perhaps already saved on your computer).
3. Go into my "Saved Projects" in Mailbox Power and make as many copies of the blank 5x7 First Touch Card (the one with the QR code) as there are houses you will be prospecting for that day. (Seven prospects? Make seven copies.)
4. Open one of your newly created copies and under "Photos" upload all of the photos of the houses for that day. You can do this one at a time but it saves a little time to just upload them all at once.
5. Drag and drop the photo of the house you are prospecting to the front of the card and to the envelope.
6. Click "Add to Cart."
7. In the cart click "Select Recipients."
8. Click "Add A Contact."
9. Input the contact information of the owner from the public record with two important adjustments:

a. Check the box to include them in the "Expired Listing Marketing" Group.

b. Put the property address in "Merge Field 1." I do this for every single house, even if the mailing address and the property address are the same. The way these letters are formatted means that the system will differentiate between mailing address and property address, but only if it is configured this way.

10. Click "Save Contact."
11. Select the recipient (it should be the person you just added who will appear right at the top of the list).
12. Click "Checkout."
13. Then move on to the next house you will be prospecting, repeating this process starting at step four. Continue until you've added every house for that day to your automation.

I used to do all of this work by hand (printing the letters and envelopes, signing, folding, stuffing, stamping, etc.) and it was slow and time-consuming. I have generated a tremendous amount of business from this technique (one client has referred me clients whose sales have totaled over $7,000,000 in business). What I really like about combining it with Mailbox Power is it allows me to prospect a large group of people over a long period of time with very little effort on my part. With practice you can have it down so you can add someone to the automation in under three minutes (depending on your internet speed), thus adding another spoke to your lead generation wheel.

Check out the reference guide at the back of the book if you are interested in obtaining any of the letters or cards in a "done for you" format as well.

FOR SALE BY OWNER (FSBOs)

It is time for a reality check. I have never sold a For Sale by Owner. The truth of the matter is they simply are not that prevalent in my area. I know, I know. One of the most common excuses people use when evaluating a new marketing system is "that will never work in my area." And yet we have found time and time again that if something works in one place, it will work in most places.

For reference, I just did a quick Zillow search for FSBOs in Los Angeles County and found 56—in a city of 10 million! So perhaps a better way to put it is, I have never been willing to put the work in to uncover the FSBOs in my market. Mastering my SOI marketing as well as expired prospecting (and now REOs! Look for that in the revised version of this book!) have kept me busy and profitable enough that I simply have not had to dig too deep in this well.

This remains an exceptionally lucrative way to generate new business, however, IF you are so inclined and IF you are in an area where there are many FSBOs. There is a system that many of my colleagues within both the eXp Realty world and the Mailbox Power world have been using to great success and, although I don't have firsthand experience with it, I want to give you a brief outline of the system as it is such a profitable source of business. And I am happy to direct to appropriate resources should you want to pursue this.

Many of the benefits of using Mailbox Power to prospect expired listings also apply to FSBO listings. This is a system you can implement across a wide variety of properties and locations with minimal effort and time required. You simply create (see the reference guide with this book for additional resources) the marketing automation, identify your prospects, and then add them to the marketing automation. At that point the system manages the creating and sending of all the marketing pieces, which frees you up to work your active deals and pursue other avenues of business.

The basic design of the system focuses on sending a series of cards and postcards emphasizing the flexible commission structure available to sellers, depending on where the buyer originates. Many (most?) owners who decide to market their homes themselves do so because they are looking to avoid paying a commission to a licensed salesperson. They believe that this money will simply be added to their bottom line. What they fail to realize, of course, is that the potential buyer is doing the same calculation except they are saying, "The seller doesn't have to pay the commission so we can just knock that cost off the price!" This creates a bit of a "double dip" situation, if you will. However, this desire to save on a commission does create an opportunity to get your foot in the door and demonstrate your expertise, flexibility, and service-oriented business approach.

The flexible commission structure works as follows. I will break it down based on the commissions in my area. You should adjust your amounts according to the norms of your market.

There are three options presented to the seller.

OPTION 1 – FSBO

In this option they continue as they are. No input, help, or support from any agents. They market their home on their own and on the off chance they find a buyer, they negotiate the deal themselves.

OPTION 2 – THE FSBO MLS

With this option you would input the property into the MLS and help the seller with the paperwork. The seller agrees to pay a 1% commission for these services, and an additional 3% commission IF another agent brings the buyer. The seller handles all the showings and communication with the other agent and/or buyer, with minimal input from you beyond administrative support to process paperwork.

OPTION 3 – THE FSBO FULL-SERVICE SELLER

This is for sellers who are ready to list with a full-time real estate professional. It includes all the bells and whistles with the following adjustment to the traditional compensation structure. If you as the listing agent bring your own buyer then the total commission is 4% (rather than the full fare 5%, 6%, or 7%). If another agent brings the buyer, then the seller pays a full commission, to be split as is customary in your area (in LA it is generally 50/50).

The most effective way to administer this marketing system is to divide your market into price points. The lower price points will receive marketing for eight weeks, while the higher price points will receive marketing for 16 weeks. You will create a FSBO automation linked to a FSBO group. Then all you need to do is add your prospective FSBOs to the group and the system will take care of the rest.

Open the Mailbox Power site and go into your saved projects. This part will be similar to the expired listing prospecting. You will be sending a series of 4X6 postcards and 5X7 greeting cards. Copy the blank template of each and add the property photo to the front of these copies. Or, if you have an Executive Membership with Mailbox Power, simply save the property photo with each contact and then use the Photo Merge feature to the cover of each, customized to each seller.

Now move to the automation builder. Create a new automation and name it after the property address. Then build the automation in the following progression:

Touch 1 – 5X7 Greeting Card

Touch 2 – 4X6 Postcard

Touch 3 – 4X6 Postcard

Touch 4 – 4X6 Postcard

Touch 5 – 5X7 Greeting Card

Touch 6 – 4X6 Postcard

Touch 7 – 4X6 Postcard

Touch 8 – 4X6 Postcard

If this is a house in the higher price point you simply repeat this pattern for an additional eight touches. They should be scheduled to go out every fourth day. The idea here is you want the seller to receive the cards and postcards on Mondays (after what has most likely been a disappointing open house over the weekend) and on Thursdays (as they are beginning to think about the upcoming weekend's activity).

Once you've created the automation (see the resources list if you'd like to have this done for you) go to your address book and create a group called "FSBO Prospects." Enroll this group in the FSBO automation you've just created.

Now all you need to do is add your prospects to this group and the system will do all the follow up for you. It is recommended you schedule two definite times a week to administer this system. You should get current on the prospects already on the list (who has decided not to sell, who has decided to list with an agent, and who is still going it alone), and then do your research to add new people to the list.

The power of this system is it allows you to prospect a large number of people over a substantial period of time with minimal effort on your part. This way you can constantly be growing your list of potential clients on autopilot, which frees you up to tend to your existing business.

So there you have it.

These four tried and true areas of perennial business will always bear fruit if you become consistent and professional about how you are engaging with each of these different groups. Whether it's the phone, door knocking, or a system like Mailbox Power, IF you continually polish these skills and keep working, I have faith that you can achieve whatever real estate dreams your heart desires.

ABOUT THE AUTHOR

Rusty Hamrick brings to the table nearly 25 years of experience in real estate sales. With a breadth of experience spanning studio condos to multi-million-dollar homes, standard sales to foreclosures, bankruptcy situations to probate court sales, there isn't a situation he hasn't tackled. Rusty started at one of the "Big Box" real estate companies before moving to the preeminent boutique agency in the Los Angeles area. Later he became the training director for the Beverly Hills Keller Williams during their opening years. He took a brief hiatus from the real estate game to open a drug and alcohol treatment center in Hollywood. While they were able to help many people, Rusty jokes that working in the treatment world has given him "a newfound appreciation for the peace and quiet of real estate!" He returned to the real estate world just as the recovery from the recession was beginning, eventually moving his license to eXp Realty—the second-best business decision he's ever made (right behind using Mailbox Power!). He is excited to share his years of expertise with anyone interested in starting or upping their real estate game!

Made in the USA
Monee, IL
04 November 2026

67388642R10059